THE PRAYING ATHLETE
QUOTE BOOK

VOL 1

PLAYING
THE GAME

Unless otherwise indicated, Scripture quotations in this
book are taken from The Holy Bible, *New International
Version®, NIV®.* Copyright © 1973, 1978, 1984, 2011
by Biblica, Inc.™ Used by permission. All rights reserved
worldwide.

Published by The Core Media Group, Inc., P.O. Box 2037,
Indian Trail, NC 28079.

Cover & Interior Design: Ashlyn Helms

Printed in the United States of America.

VOL 1 PLAYING THE GAME

Many times in life we have to be patient and let the game melt into our focus. You cannot force something that is not there. Power versus Power only makes for a collision. Find the right window and then burst through it with excitement and power to find the green grass, daylight, and celebration—the End Zone!

"A hot-tempered person stirs up conflict, but the one who is patient calms a quarrel."
Proverbs 15:18

One day, one game or one play,
whether good or bad, shall never
define my heart or my God-given
talents. I press on, prepare and
plan for the next game, the next
play, and the next day. This
is what I can control: the
preparation and focus on what is
ahead. This day is done and
cannot be changed. I have
embraced what I learned today
and now it is behind me.

"Not that I have already obtained all
this, or have already arrived at my goal,
but I press on to take hold of that for
which Christ Jesus took hold of me."
Philippians 3:12

People look up to athletes as role models. Use your talents as a platform to promote the One who gifted you.

"Whoever claims to live in him must live as Jesus did."
1 John 2:6

**Eight ways to build confidence in
competition:
1- Stay focused on what you
want to achieve.
2- Train with a plan.
3- Play with passion.
4- Fight to win, not survive.
5- Be purposeful in your goals
and direction.
6- Master your skills.
7- Overcome distractions.
8- Do nothing to delay
your dream.**

"For the Lord will at your side and will
keep your foot from being snared."
Proverbs 3:26

There is a difference between winning championships and being a champion.

"For everyone born of God overcomes the world. This is the victory that has overcome the world, even our faith. Who is it that overcomes the world? Only the one who believes that Jesus is the Son of God."
1 John 5:4-5

If you think you will have a great season, you are probably right. If you think you will have bad season, you are probably right. What we believe dictates the reality we live in.

"Truly I tell you, if anyone says to this mountain, 'Go throw yourself into the sea,' and does not doubt in their heart but believes that what they say will happen, it will be done for them."
Mark 11:23

**Step toward your inner self to
find peace of mind and
confidence to win.**

"You will keep in perfect peace those
whose minds are steadfast, because
they trust in you."
Isaiah 26:3

Perfection will always be paralyzing, and limit your potential, until you realize perfection is really pressing toward a goal that can only be chased and never caught.

"Indeed, there is no one on earth who is righteous, no one who does what is right and never sins."
Ecclesiastes 7:20

As you engage yourself in game day remember this: OPEN, O = ONE, P= PLAY, E=EXECUTE, N= NOW. Write it down so you can see it and then believe in it. "OPEN" is a focus factor to achieve success on the field. If you stay focused on what happened during the play before, or what could happen next, or how you are feeling, you have lost your ability to excel on the current play. Focus on the current play, which is 3-6 seconds. Embrace "OPEN" and it will change your mental performance to enhance your physical performance.

"For if the willingness is there, the gift is acceptable according to what one has, not according to what one does not have."
2 Corinthians 8:12

Sometimes there is a voice
telling you to quit now and avoid
failure, and telling you that
success is impossible. Don't
listen to this voice. If you put
everything into what you are
striving for, you could make it.
Quitting before you try will bring
a heavy heart of dissatisfaction,
and you will always find yourself
asking the question, "What if...?"
Don't ever doubt yourself. Stay
the course. Pray, Work, Believe,
and Be Confident! Go out and
play the game with
passion and desire.

"Let us not become weary in doing
good, for at the proper time we will
reap a harvest if we do not give up."
Galatians 6:9

Play each game as if it is your first and your last. You will find gratitude that you can play and sadness that the game will soon be over. This combination creates enthusiasm for the moment.

"And whatever you do, whether in word or deed, do it all in the name of the Lord Jesus, giving thanks to God the Father through him."
Colossians 3:17

Passion will lead you to success. Lack of passion leads you nowhere. Bring passion for the game you love.

Whatever you do, work at it with all your heart, as working for the Lord, not for human masters."
Colossians 3:23

Don't pray for a win, thank God for a chance to compete.

"Give thanks in all circumstances; for this is God's will for you in Christ Jesus."
1 Thessalonians 5:18

**Maintain a high level of
confidence in your skill set.
Never allow others to take what
you already own. It is your
confidence, not theirs,
so keep ownership of it.**

"So do not throw away your confidence;
it will be richly rewarded. You need to
persevere so that when you have done
the will of God, you will receive
what he has promised."
Hebrews 10:35-36

**Building confidence is a
two-step process:
1- Stop thinking.
2- Start Believing.**

"Therefore I tell you, whatever you
ask for in prayer, believe that you have
received it, and it will be yours."
Mark 11:24

Play for the love you have for the game, not for the love the game gives you.

"For where your treasure is, there your heart will be also."
Matthew 6:21

Work your wins into existence.

"A sluggard's appetite is never filled,
but the desires of the diligent
are fully satisfied."
Proverbs 13:4

**Winning today is
much more important than
winning yesterday.**

"The Lord has done it this very day; let
us rejoice today and be glad."
Psalm 118:24

**Always play for the outcome:
the love of the game, the
passion to do what you love.
Never play for the income.
If you play for the outcome, the
income will surpass your own
thoughts and dreams.**

"Do you not know that in a race all
the runners run, but only one gets the
prize? Run in such a way as to get the
prize. Everyone who competes in the
games goes into strict training. They do
it to get a crown that will not last,
but we do it to get a crown
that will last forever."
1 Corinthians 9:24-25

Your skill set is an art, but an artist who does not perform may lose those skills. Practice often.

"Watch out that you do not lose what we have worked for, but that you may be rewarded fully."
2 John 1:8

Difficult practices make for easy games.

"Blessed is the one who perseveres under trial because, having stood the test, that person will receive the crown of life that the Lord has promised to those who love him."

James 1:12

**Be focused on what you can do
for the game and the game
will reward you.**

"Commit to the Lord whatever you do,
and he will establish your plans."
Proverbs 16:3

Don't dwell on the wins and losses of the past. The most important game of your life is the next one.

"Forget the former things; do not dwell on the past. See, I am doing a new thing! Now it springs up; do you not perceive it? I am making a way in the wilderness and streams in the wasteland."
Isaiah 43:18-19

Often times we wish we could retake our last shot and give it another try. The game is unforgiving, but that doesn't mean you have to be as well. Always give people a second chance.

"Be kind and compassionate to one another, forgiving one another, just as in Christ God forgave you."
Ephesians 4:32

You can undo some things in life, but you cannot undo the scoreboard.

"For all have sinned and fall short of the glory of God."
Romans 3:23

If the player you are is not the player you want to be, stop making excuses and work toward who you want to become.

"Blessed is the one who does not walk in step with the wicked or stand in the way that sinners take or sit in the company of mockers, but whose delight is in the law of the Lord, and who meditates on his law day and night."
Psalm 1:1-2

If your goal is only to be better than the next guy, you are limiting yourself from what you can achieve.

"If anyone thinks they are something they are not, they deceive themselves. Each one should test their own actions. Then they can take pride in themselves alone, without comparing themselves to someone else, for each one should carry their own load."
Galatians 6:3-5

**Getting there is hard.
Staying there is harder.
Being there is a blessing.**

"But as for you, be strong and do not
give up, for your work will
be rewarded."
2 Chronicles 15:7

A comeback is dependent on you.

"Now to him who is able to do immeasurably more than all we ask or imagine, according to his power that is at work within us..."
Ephesians 3:20

**Challenges will come and go;
when they come, just press on.
The storm always ends.**

"I consider that our present sufferings
are not worth comparing with the glory
that will be revealed in us."
Romans 8:18

THOUGHTS & REFLECTIONS

_____

_____

_____

_____

_____

_____

_____

_____

_____

_____

_____

_____

_____

_____

_____

_____

_____

_____

_____

_____

_____

_____

_____

_____

_____

_____

_____

_____

_____

_____

_____

_____

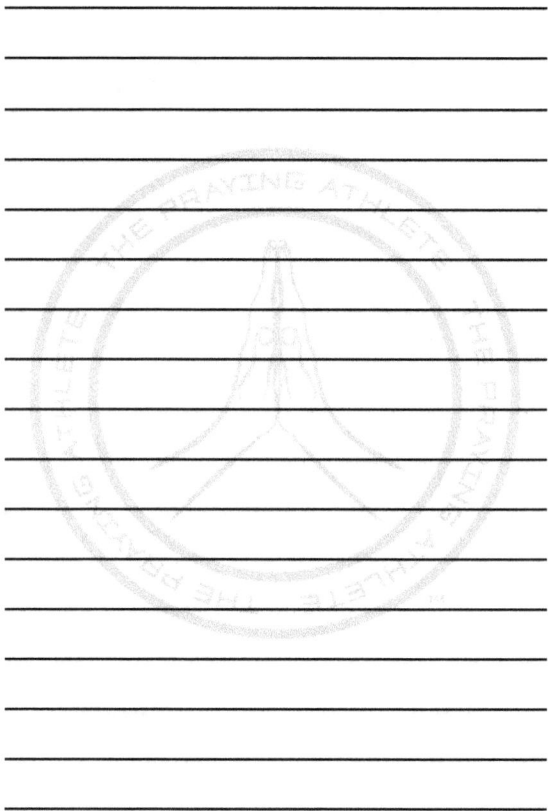

_____

_____

_____

_____

_____

_____

_____

_____

_____

_____

_____

_____

_____

_____

_____

_____

_____

_____

_____

_____

_____

_____

_____

_____

_____

_____

_____

_____

_____

_____

_____

_____

_____

_____

MY QUOTES

_____

_____

_____

_____

_____

_____

_____

_____

_____

_____

_____

_____

_____

_____

_____

_____

_____

_____

_____

_____

_____

_____

_____

_____

_____

_____

_____

_____

_____

_____

_____

ACKNOWLEDGEMENTS

I want to acknowledge and say thank you to all those that
helped with this project:

Nadia Guy
Ashlyn Helms
My Mom & Dad

All of my NFL Clients, current and former, that have
encouraged me to share these words with others.

ABOUT
TPA

The Praying Athlete is a movement that creates an organic culture of prayer through an uplifting community and authentic conversation.

For more information, visit our website **www.theprayingathlete.com**.

Follow us on social media.

@ThePrayingAthlete

@Praying_Athlete

@ThePrayingAthlete

COLLECT ALL
8 VOL.

Our first volume of *The Praying Athlete Quote Book* addresses the topic of playing the game. Quotes and thoughts from Robert B. Walker, paired with Scripture from God's Word, allow readers to get a good idea about what playing a good game looks like.

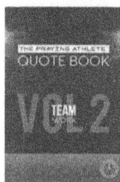

Our second volume of *The Praying Athlete Quote Book* addresses the topic of teamwork. Quotes and thoughts from Robert B. Walker, paired with Scripture from God's Word, allow readers to understand what it means to be a good teammate and surround yourself with people who lift you up.

Our third volume of *The Praying Athlete Quote Book* addresses the topic of growth & preparation for the future. Quotes and thoughts from Robert B. Walker, paired with Scripture from God's Word, allow readers to know that even though the future is uncertain, there is a plan and purpose for everyone.

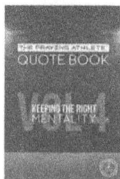

Our fourth volume of *The Praying Athlete Quote Book* addresses the topic of keeping the right mentality. Quotes and thoughts from Robert B. Walker allow readers to understand how staying in the right mindset can improve overall performance.

Our fifth volume of *The Praying Athlete Quote Book* addresses the topic of staying motivated. Quotes and thoughts from Robert B. Walker allow readers to become motivated to accomplish their goals, even when they feel they are not up to the task.

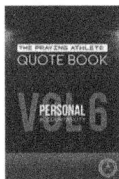

Our sixth volume of *The Praying Athlete Quote Book* addresses the topic of personal accountability. Quotes and thoughts from Robert B. Walker allow readers to think about how they can better themselves. Whether its ending a bad habit or saying no to anything that may hurt themselves or others, staying accountable will benefit one's character and performance.

Our seventh volume of *The Praying Athlete Quote Book* addresses the topic of living life. This volume is the first part in a two part living life series. Quotes and thoughts from Robert B. Walker give readers a better understanding of how to live life to the fullest.

Our eighth volume of *The Praying Athlete Quote Book* addresses the topic of living life. This volume is the second part in a two part living life series. Quotes and thoughts from Robert B. Walker give readers a better understanding of how to live life to the fullest.

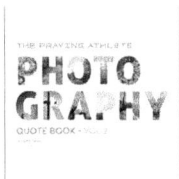

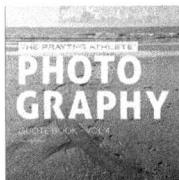

www.ingramcontent.com/pod-product-compliance
Lightning Source LLC
Chambersburg PA
CBHW071745020426
42331CB00008B/2192